NOBLE REMNANTS

Published by Dreaming Deer Press

Marietta, GA, USA 30067

ISBN-13: 9780692636404

ISBN-10: 0692636404

Cover art by Emily Lupita, watercolor & ink, 2004.

Printed in the United States of America

For poetry books, CDs & DVDs
by Joseph S. Plum, please visit:

www.JoePlum.com

Noble Remnants

Joseph S. Plum

Preface

The poems written in this book were transcribed from the original oral poetry that was crafted in the bardic tradition of dreaming and living a lifetime in connection with nature. The hope is that by writing down the poems and collecting them into books, they may travel widely and be shared with the world. If you have a chance, please say these poems aloud. In this way, the beauty and power of traditional bardic poetry will live on through your voice.

Artist's Statement

spirit winds are blowing

passing over the tree of life

small brown leaves are falling

turning into children running

across this Earth

laughing as they go!

-Joseph Samuel Plum

from *twilight breath*

Contents

for Air

chant down

look
   light now is coming
darkness is ending
   the soul fire is drumming
shadows are dancing
   treetops are chanting
with strange tongues clicking
   far away tomorrow
a message is sending
   look to the sky
a dream now is bending
   stepping from the stars
spirits are descending
   in our hearts
a pathway is open
   with quick thoughts
welcome is spoken
   gone with the rhythm
of a crossing just chosen
   together a home visit
to forever dwelling

here is the moment
of ancient feel touching
there is a taste
of spirit wind blowing
where are the children
bright eyed and excited ?
(playing with the old one
no longer sleeping)
see the spark
in the eyes of the living
noble remnant
all futures weave

a fire is drumming
treetops are chanting
far away tomorrow
with us is dancing

here now memory
another day's promise
there now tomorrow
powerfully pulling

where now the voice
calling us softly?
  in liquid oblivion
 action clear
    first in the air
all around us
    then in the breath
swirling inside
    here now in a whisper
surging to attention
    there now in the silence
of watching tears fall
    look into the darkness
of beyond life knowing
    look
light now is coming!

oracle

just as these words
are like smoke
so the same
my heart is a fire
it's a blood
of forest and wind
that i require
or else as ash
to this earth
i'll soon retire
my crackling flame burnt
of its own desire
without wood and air
i have no choice
no mouth to give
my breath this voice
no sounds to ring
and echo in the mind
bringing forth from silence
many thoughts divine

in the wildness

where wisdom grows

there is a tree

whose fruit

no one knows

on a branch

that separates

day from night

there sleeps there

in solitude

a many splendid delight

among the stones

who have grown

cold and dark

there awaits there

a hidden silver spark

a tongue of light

not yet to be

a birthless blaze

of unmatched poetry.

down a tunnel

of spirit wings

through a soundfall

of translucent dreams

above and beyond

all earthly things

heaven loves

a wind that sings.

    turn

and greet the sky

where it meets the earth

pour out your feelings

for all their worth

then stay

to touch the hills

as they grow dark

to cry as though

you've lost you heart

blood, hair, flesh, and bone

together

these become as nothing

when the very next wind that blows

comes to claim your breath

for its very own.

nightwatch

curve of yellow

rimmed with darkness

blue horizon set below

we are the children

of no tomorrow

and we've come to claim

your temples as our home

we bring with us

a pledge of honor

and the valley spirit

from which we've grown

for we are born perpetual

out of joy and sorrow

on the winds

where seeds are sown

in us

high and deep

can come together

bringing into being

each other on their own

like day and night

we must travel in tandem

to and from a time unknown

just beyond your range of vision

one hundred warriors

are waking in a dream

gathering strength

they raise their weapons

by centering

while side-stepping

into the main flow

of your conscious stream

    in our native

mountainous nether regions

as the night watch returns to dawn

campfires of five thousand generations

are being extinguished

replaced by the presence of the sun

at the end of every tunnel vision

deepening shadows are swallowed

one by one

while from the mouth

of those who are believing

each breath issues forth

a wondrous stream of song.

    awake now from within

the sleeping giant

whose throat has long been

a cave to medicine men

gather the harvest of healing power

that's been kept there waiting

clinched in the crystal teeth of the wind

this earth is a beauty

alive with feeling

enthroned without beginning

in a time which has no end

where in a dreamscape barren

and windswept of virtue

alone we must wander

until love takes us

into an awakening

from which our own death

becomes a friend.

embryo nation

now
i don't know who here
will agree with me
sometimes though it seems
as if the greatest part of each of us
actually exists elsewhere
and what you know of me
and what i see of you
is simply the smallest portion
of a much larger, greater whole
therefore when we gather together
(as we have here today)
through our thoughts
and through our feelings
we bring into being
into these realms
those who actually exist elsewhere.
     yes, today is for the ones
who wait between the gates
where the inner city secret
meets the world of fates

where the unformed energies

of the embryo race

first begin to accumulate

into a sense of being

that memory can illuminate

once pure light begins to illustrate

the qualities which make life great

for we are all born children of the air

then brought to earth by uncertain despair

where we must now spin and weave

and contemplate

endeavor to outmaneuver

our earthly fate

    where is the village

of the dwellers within ?

home to the weavers of the weft

and the transformer of men

where are the steps leading

into the temple at the hollows of the wind

where the white star warrior waits

for time to begin again

as an ocean of tides laps against the sky

at this world lands end

and the lords, and the ladies

from the realm of no dominion

drift off into sleep listening

for the footfalls of their long gone

yet never quite forgotten friends

    where is this village of the dwellers within?

if you seek to belong to a time half-remembered

in answer to the urgings of your future kin

then enter now through the sound and the service

of the circle eternal

to be drawn into the open center

of the universal internal

and therein stand

to be made welcome

by the birthless assemblage

from the starlight tribes

midnight clan!

clans of midnight

greetings

from the starlight tribes

clans of midnight

i am the assembler

of the prospect of the notion

the enchanter

of worlds yet unspoken

the weaver

of a web whose thread

passes through me unbroken

the articulated embodiment

of unexpressed emotion

the leveler who comes here

with heart and hands wide open

for yes, i am the assembler

i am the fifth portion

who has gathered the seeds

that have been eons in the sowing

who has captured the thoughts

which keep the knower from the knowing

who has harvested the silence

from which these words keep on flowing

that through hearing

understanding may lead

into a feeling which is forever showing

infallible instinct to be the source

of all things alive and growing

greetings

from the starlight tribes

clans of midnight.

twilight reign

on this earth

our feet are resting

in the distance

our eyes have settled

across the horizon

our thoughts are now reclining

oh, how the crickets

and little frogs were singing

in those first days

of an early autumn

winter's silence

came soon upon them

they could feel

the cold night returning

beneath the leaves

they stayed on their journeys

while here on the earth

their feet were resting

who will listen

for you at sunset

and carry your shadow

towards the dawn

no one knows

the steps you have taken

or the way i will

greet the sun

when beneath the clouds

on a mountain of dreams

our feet are resting

as the twilight reign begins

while in the fields below

the homeless are whispering

to each other in the wind

they say that the green

is all too quickly leaving

that their time in this world

has reached an end

then turning to me

with gentle faces

they ask

will you not come with us

into the heartland

of all places

and watch

as our children drop

from beneath our skin

do you not know

the voice of remembering

that leads across

a threshold

into the home

of the wolf

who is a friend

you do not know

that here on this earth

our feet are resting

while far away

into the future

our spirits have been

to teach ourselves

the songs

the little ones are singing

that we might call them

back from the silence again

when on the edge of extinction

we travel together

to clear out the pathways

for the passing
of a few true men.

all but forgotten
this forever dwelling
this horseless rider
whose heart is galloping
towards the ragged throats
of winter
never begotten
by skillful arguing
this childlike offering
which insists on telling
of prenatal ancient beginnings
underlying
every physical sensation
undying
in the face of seasonal change
time out of mind
we will again become blessed
as we become "us"
once ignited by design
the light in the eyes

of the unnamed one

flames up.

    born of the blood

of burning desire

on the tip of my tongue

is the taste of fire

as these words each turn

to ashes then dust

birth follows death

as always it must

spoken in the hopes

of renewing a vow

while drawing shade

out of shadow

a language of light

was released somehow

it was a question of harmony

focused on a movement within

and although

the answer was balance

the solution

is brought about

by listening

to the gospels of the wind.

    alone

each of us has been left to find

a thread that unravels

the fabric of space and time

not to be afraid

is very hard to do

when heaven and earth

in all their might

have made only one of you

as the momentum of generations

begins to unwind

the spirit who moves

steps forward to redefine

the principle commitment

that connects body to mind

and then shadows

from the moon and the sun

shall overlap

while the multitudes from creation

speak up

on their own behalf

so that after the touch

of those who are

much more than us

all that remains

to be expressed

is that in the old gods

the young ones must trust.

    no dream nor fantasy

or unspoken desire

can bring to the forefront

the virtues of fire

like sleeping in the cold

in concert

with being hungry and tired

no fable nor metaphor

or mythological past

can sanctify ritual into a feeling

that the heart can grasp

unless first rooted in heavens

and then in blood held fast

for truth entertains no notion

that will not last.

forward leaping eye

dark night

no wind

just out of sight

walks

a traveler within,

though breathless passage

may ease the soul,

still

mirrored in tears

ancient pain

frames boundless portions

of the whole.

spin about!

grab at the prospect,

freedom permits

perpetual anguish to burn

stone bound on a beach of time

for the forward leaping eye can see

looking back from the future

children of eternity

wrapped

in blankets of invisibility.

cast in the mother tongue

of whispered revelations

in the dark

seasons passing speak directly

through change

liberating feelings held captive

in the heart

imagine awakening into a time

whose every moment

is a movement

towards living life as art,

a world

where each light beam can be seen

bringing spirit beings in singing

from afar.

in the heavens unseen

there are forces

who play upon us

like fingers on a string,

deep in the heart

of the human dream

there sleeps keynotes of memory

that when struck

give rise

to a music of fluid beauty

emerging with creativity

through fountains of energy

to purify our conscious stream.

truly someday

we shall all be born

again together

from beneath

this blue sky belly of our mother

in body and mind

twin flames of a single candle

burning brightly forever

in heart and spirit,

dual shards of dawn's light

splintering the darkness

into brilliant surrender

as the great-grandchildren

of the sleeper in time

awake

with the advent of insight

and begin to remember

a pathway of light that leads

through a forest of burning embers

where the smoke of indifference

stems from a pain of remembrance

and the one true way

of embryonic enlightenment

leads through a day sun

of unequalled enchantment

whose mother is the total

of all that has gone before us

and whose father

is a forceful feeling

pulling us through every tomorrow

into a moment whose existence

is the source of all things born

of joys and of sorrow.

together with a hope

pressed closely from within

and a promise of finding a land

which knows no sin,

we have wandered

like phantoms before the wind

and together we have looked

over the edge

of a boundless, fertile sea

to find ourselves alone

each one of us

a living, breathing

island

of vibrant

timeless reality.

yes, the forward leaping eye can see!

star sight

hollow
rings the echo
around these sovereign hills
at night
    bright the eyes
of the wandering children
grown older
rimmed with liquid firelight
    broken
is the hoop of willow
bent beyond bounds
by destiny's awesome might
when spoken is the will
of the shining blue icon
each word sparkling
with refracted star sight
    swift are the thoughts
which fly like arrows
into the rising belly of night
cutting away
at this side of darkness

with eyes that flash

like the edge of a knife

    great is the wind

as it sweeps down the narrows

clearing out clutter

from a compromised life

creating an air

charged with potential

one just right

for breathless flight

    where are the dreams

which gather like rainbows?

sweet children

of ambition's furious might

are they high above us?

weaving an anthem of color

a banner

whose promise spans

the bulk of our lives

    there is a way

which leads into seeing

beyond the memories

that screen out original sight

it is here among us

hidden in the depths of believing

we truly know the difference

between wrong and right

   for soft are the steps

of the life force ascending

into the twilight vapors

of a primordial sky

where broken by increments

into constricted potential

long ago love

in the ancient ways

stopped flowing

and gave the rest

of eternity the time

to pass us on by

    now we are like islands

surrounded by oceans

now we are like clouds

climbing out of the sea

now we are like starlight

waiting for darkness

holding

to a power in our hearts
that can set this world free
    look to the landscape
for a view in the morning
gaze into the eyes
of this earth at your feet
carry the moment
like a child who is hungry
alive with feeling
that tomorrow might be

    near is the day
which moves into feeling
a vertical departure
from the lateral fields
spiraling ascension
into stunning retention
as the oscillating aspects of duality
begin to congeal
    go with the voices
returning to wholeness
join with the warriors
who no longer compete

trust in the future

with a heart full of freedom

longing to sustain

but never repeat

    here is the way

that leaps into being

there is the platform

at the base of our feet

here is today

in the service of tomorrow

what more could we need

to be complete ?

paradigm creed

do you believe in seeds
planted in wild places,
in the taste of river mist
and the smell of sages?
do you believe in mountains
while crossing the borderline
and bridges in the desert
spanning the depths of time?
do you believe in the journey of a soul,
in destinations made manifest
by the dreams and visions that we hold?
do you believe in a spirit life
fashioned by design
stretching across a threshold
created by leaving autonomy behind?
do you believe in sunlight
filtering through green leaves
and in the shadows of untold winters
hugging the branches of trees?
yes, there is a pathway
extending from this moment at hand

enduring throughout eternity

in the heart and breath of man.

   do you believe in an open gate

and radiant splendor,

in engagements ongoing

which struggle to surrender

meaning to solitude

and the ability to engender

space without time

empowered

with the impulse to remember

human beings as children

and pure light

as the great defender

of a faith that is defined

until finally freed

by a mind which accepts

then releases the paradigm creed?

tell me,
please tell me,
do you believe?
do you believe in seeds
planted in wild places?

on the way

on the way to myself

there is no path

beneath my feet

above my head

no sky

on the way

who is it that stops to stare

while in blindness

all others pass on by

on the way

where is the voice

to lift up the prayer

which begs no pardon in reply

but asks rather

for a heartfelt tear

to wipe clean

the corners of my eye

on the way

who is it that sets off

in the morning light

but never, ever arrives

beyond the breakwater

of that midnight moment

which separates this

from all my other lives

    on the way

why should my heavenly father care

if i live or if i die

for does not the great ocean mother

we each share

receive all rivers

regardless of her tides?

    on the way

am i not blind

because i hear

deaf when i see

thoughtless if i feel

and am i not myself

because i am on the way?

relics
    (event horizon)

      i know
that my knowing
separates me from my being
and that being
keeps me from becoming
and that becoming
is but dusty powder made
by grinding here and there
together.

      therefore it is said:
these are the days of passage
under the sign of the promise given
now is the time to call to mind
the terms of the bargain driven
between the earthen blood from man
and the starlight tribes of heaven
within the ancient belly
of our ancestral sky
a new constellation has arisen.

a confluence of quintessence

is beginning to align

an internal conjunction

of universal rhyme

where each gives to each

the other

as if by stellar design

for our journeys and our destinies

have become intertwined

with the hopes and dreams of people

which both mark and measure

the message

and the refinement

of human kind.

beyond the glow of twilight

on some far off distant world

among the clans of midnight

my countrymen's flags unfurled

as if from out of nowhere

on a moment's notice we come

riding the crest of another day

and into the valley of doing undone

beneath the veil of our life-long dream

below the flow of this conscious stream

wrapped in feelings for the unseen

the broken ones wait for the time being.

    when in the vicinity of infinity

watching heaven's stars fall

while throughout the certainty of eternity

most any heartbeat can recall

an equation of creation

that if brought to full resolve

brings about a balance

to the blood that is in us all.

    this air that moves

the clouds about the sky

which fills our lungs with breath

when as babies we first cry

that lays down the laws

upon which all our senses rely

this air that moves

will in time decide

if our earthly presence can survive

gravity's touch at evening's tide.

    yet in the sparkle

that comes from our eyes

there is a fire

which lights up the lives

of those we've left unborn

until from the fabric

of our kinship ties

just one more child

is torn.

    my ancient ancestors

arrived one day

taking my heart

in their hands

they turned away

leaving an opening

in my chest

where the sky comes to play.

out on the rim of the world

they gathered

moving like clouds

reflected in the water

on command from the wind

they scattered

until in the numbing pain

i could find

what it is they're after,

to touch the earth

is all that really matters.

    to touch the earth

with simplicity

is to turn that touching

to a litany

for in each of us

there sleeps the memory

of what it is

to simply be,

and in that being

there awakes the certainty

of the necessity of preserving

ancestral dignity

for with the beginnings

of antiquity

we became the keepers

of a legacy

that is in itself a seed

needing only to believe

in the dispersal

of impersonal gravity

and the emergence

of a fifth season

composed in its entirety

of all illuminating integrity

for in a life lived

with no guarantees

moving from body to body

the soul is forever free

at rest and unexpressed

in legion with the dawn

a procession of sensation

whose cadence depends upon

an assertive reflective position

in revolution around a sun

an odyssey of exploration

which goes on and on

a journey into folklore

that's never done,

like a fold

in a baby's blanket

or the first note

in a young child's song

it's a harvest of tomorrows

that's been here all along.
now the day of the clouds has passed
and shall not come again
seldom does the fool in us
turn quickly enough to see
what it is that the wise one
just never does.

for in this world
only shadows
may walk in balance
turning no stones
in their search for eloquence
gracefully following sunlight's request
moving in harmony
while still at rest.
ever since the time of angels
where darkness fell so quickly
relics of the past remain
to guide us on our journeys
through a once famous
but now forgotten land
born of emerging embryonic emotion
that can twist and turn

but just will not stand

unless delivered

by the prospect of the notion

that here there is more

between heaven and earth

than meets the eyes

and arms of man

more to arriving

in the afterlife

than simply leaving behind

these feelings

which lie so close at hand.

    listen to the stirrings

in your heart

mark now, this moment

as the start

of the day in whose evening

we must depart

the safe harbors

of our incomplete understanding

for we all

have inner sails that rise

on celestial winds

which come disguised

as a breath of air

in the still of night

where we wait to leave

like the fading light

though we know not

the course we're steering,

thoughts our senses

bring to mind

shall leave this shrunken world behind

for among the teachings of all mankind

there is only one lesson

that never ends in time.

    be it as it is

for it never was

is the original translation

of the forceful feeling

which flows in my blood

to pass away in lightness

on a bridge that leads

is to arrive out of darkness

set to conceive

a body born undying

at rest and in peace

in union with a spirit

who's ready to receive

a soul no longer bound

by concentric thought,

a phantom of awareness

that's never quite caught

by any convergence of paradox

around a vortex that's not

a masterful illusion

entirely self-taught

maintaining through diffusion

all the momentum of a being apart

who waits between for the conclusion

of a still-beating heart

which stops for a time in this world

while in another it starts.

    in the heavens

a pure heart is pounding

as up from silence

a once stilled pulse

 is again assembling

while out of elsewhere

an oblique sun is rising

softly over fields of gray.

is it not too surprising

that this is our different day?

the shadows are of tomorrow

that i plainly see

yet my bones are filled with sorrow

for what may never be.

    beyond the horizons of our vision

a river of light is burning

carving a valley of many thunders

through a realm of no dominion

how often have we as children

walked hand in hand with our dreaming

shaping this tomorrow

like a plaything of little meaning?

yet again today in passing

we can give no proper sign of recognition

until in the dust of death rejoining

with that sense of being enchanted

by the joys of simple childhood

where as masters of the flame

we must view entire forests

as nothing more than firewood,

and keep ourselves in waiting

for the coming of the winter

where the cold becomes a sinner

and our body's warmth the saint.

    blessed be the beast in me

when it's my head that lays upon the hillside

as my spirit waits with the trees

for the wind to come at midnight

sacred are the dreams

that smell and taste like home

great is the sacrifice of blood

which mixes with my own

holy is the dawn

in which the night hunters are returning

may the arrogance of illusion

be dissolved in the light of morning

divine is a cry from darkness

on folded wings at midday

for timeless prayer

is a child of hunger

behind whose lips

breathless words hatch

into birds of prey

circling high above

this morsel of reason

where trembling on bended knee

i know now what they'll say

deep inside the temples of tomorrow

once the gods of science have gone away.

    come!

sleep tonight upon the altar

lay there until the break of day

dream of all life has to offer

save up your courage to trade away.

strike a bargain

with your ancestral forefathers

that they may give up to you

their wisdom from beyond the grave

where for so long

they have sat and watched

from down under

at the rise and fall

of these vessels made of clay

guarding well the secrets

they will now surrender

strong and true in every way.

   these are relics

in which we're dealing

these simple words

with complex meanings

that are unconquered concepts

bound up in feelings

of minute amounts of major proportion

that are in every sense

beyond all notion.

these are relics

of the old religion

from a time

before ambition

led us astray

from a world

where there are no sins

to be forgiven

or someone else's

debt to pay

for what we are

are human becomings

in a fragmented sort of way

searching

for the proper rites of passage

among the artifacts of yesterday

while just one moment

spent in balance

could easily focus

the energy of all eternity

and bring back

with a flash of golden lightning

the most instinctive

of our creative ability

to string together

a rosary incarnate

beaded with veiled memories

each one a jeweled garment

enshrining the essence

of all our past life histories

which pour forth

from the hollows of this mortal chalice

rimmed with undying mystery

destined

to be ordained in communion

with the sacrament of this instant
where delicately woven times
pass by
like black birds
through standing trees.

    in the foothills of afterthought
a tremendous vision grows
a blossom of consuming delight:
this earth beneath our toes
blessed be our homeland
for yes, there is a mother to us all
and her name and virtue is
silence.

in unison

silver haired the lion
lays down with the sheep
not being tired or hungry
with no desire to eat
when he opens his mouth
it's simply to teach
but the lambs hear only a roar
and quickly retreat
to the safety of a flock
where every creature will agree
that to baa
is the one proper way to preach
to baa or to roar
neither one is complete
where every man is half lion
and two-thirds sheep
and the only thoughtful sound
in unison that both can reach
comes when we dream we awake
while still asleep
from the voice of a memory

who stands on its own two feet

by taking from every lesson

the impulse to receive

and giving in return a feeling

in which reason can believe

so that ourselves and our future

can be forever freed

from the struggle of a heart

afraid to bleed

for fear of the lion

who has come

to lay down

with the sheep.

cathedral spires

i have no use

for many things

and many things

have no use for me

this is the way

the way has been

ever since i was

a child of three.

a child of three

cannot help but see

the world through

a youthful point of view

so that with playfulness

and a sense of trust

a guiding light

can come shining through.

in the eye of the beholder

who will grow no older

radiant vision is daily renewed

until as a child of nine

deep in the mind

an unseen hand

closes its grip

and begins again
to move.
no one knows why
we live and we die
or how we came
into the aptitude.
it's a miracle
if we survive
long enough to decide
that inside every mirage
there lies the outline
of a truth.

   earthen mother
sky born father
wind song for baby food
out beyond
the peaks and the vistas
of the cathedral spires
eternity spreads her wings
and gathers in her brood.

About the Author

Joseph Samuel Plum is a direct descendant of Welsh bards and Native American spirit. He lives in South Central Iowa within a group of trees where he composes and presents bardic poetry of original nature. He has been doing this for fifty years. This is his seventh book.

Books by Joseph S. Plum:

RELICS

CONCENTRIC DEVOTION

LANDMASS AND OTHER POEMS

STAR SIGHT GATHERING

WHERE RISING VOICES GROW

HUMAN LANDSCAPE

NOBLE REMNANTS

BOOK OF SHADOWS

OLD PATH

www.JoePlum.com

www.ingramcontent.com/pod-product-compliance
Lightning Source LLC
Chambersburg PA
CBHW051705090426
42736CB00013B/2554